30 Ways
To Improve Your Golf

By

Peter Dangerfield
PGA Golf Professional
www.peterdangerfield.myprogolfer.co.uk

Shield Crest

ISBN 978-1-907629-15-0

MMXI

Published by
ShieldCrest
Aylesbury, Buckinghamshire, HP22 5RR
www.shieldcrest.co.uk

Acknowledgements

Many thanks to the Manager of Minchinhampton Golf Club Old Course Alan Dangerfield, Shop Assistants John Giles and Barry Coombs for their photographic skills used in the countless swing takes and retakes.

To the members of Minchinhampton Old Course and New Course who continually encouraged me to write "Peter`s Pro Pointers" for The Stroud Life local weekly paper and thereafter stating I should publish a book.

The Minchinhampton Golf Club Old and New Courses for allowing me access for on course photography.

A special mention to all the Danish Golfers that I have had the pleasure of teaching during my 25 years incredible journey around many parts of beautiful Denmark. The wonderful Golf Clubs of Gilleleje, Fureso, Herning, Korsor, Koge and Sydsjaellands .

To Lene my dear Wife who managed the shops at all the Golf Courses named above (spending many long hours setting up a beautifully presented and well stocked shop). Lene also endured many isolated evenings alone as I locked myself away in the home office writing my Pro Pointers. As she always states; "What will be the next project" – maybe volume two of this book?

Finally to you the reader – I trust you will gain an understanding of all the golf swing issues that have been discussed and illustrated in my book. My sincere hope is that your handicap will be reduced because of the knowledge you have found.

About The Author

Peter Dangerfield has been teaching golf for 35 years starting in Denmark in 1976 as an Assistant Professional at Fureso & Gilleleje Golf Klubs for a 2 year period. This followed Head Professional positions at Korsor for 3 years, Herning for 8 years and Gilleleje for 12 years. During his time in Denmark he served on the Danish PGA Committee as Cashier and Instructor for Assistants.

In 2001 he rejoined his Junior Club Minchinhampton Old Course in Gloucestershire, England and in 2010 set up an Indoor Teaching Academy with all the latest video technology. A burning desire to continue teaching golf at the highest standard has resulted in his selection as a coach to the newly formed Gloucestershire Junior Academy.

Having coached all types of players from complete beginners to tournament professionals, he is a much respected teacher. Peter has given over 50,000 lessons during his career and quotes;

"My aim is not to give you something I have - but to reveal to you something you already possess!".

Having written over 80 "Peter`s Pro Pointers for Stroud Life", Peter wishes to share a selection of 30 in this first publication. Peter says;

"Enjoy the read, study the illustrations and become a better golfer".

Introduction

Golf is probably the most frustrating sport imaginable in that it is just between you, the player, a static ball and the golf course. What makes one golfer better than another is partially an innate skill. However, most often it`s the way one players applies him/herself to the game compared to another. Each player is different and each golf course is different. What eventually makes a lower handicap player is the time taken to study how to deal with the many different situations that arise during a round of golf.

Having written over 80 Lessons for a local newspaper "Stroud Life" Peter decided he wanted to share his knowledge with a wider audience. After much soul searching, he has chosen these 30 lessons.

Most golfers want to see their handicap reduced and in this first book, Peter Dangerfield highlights the most common problems encountered by golfers during a round and how to deal with them. Also included are some common swing problems that can arise even for the better player.

Peter says:

"These 30 Lessons successfully applied, will inevitably result in a handicap reduction."

30 of Peter's Best Tips To Improve Your Game and Reduce Your Handicap

The Wrist Break and Presetting

Players can have the perfect grip, posture and set up. However, if the arms and body do not work in harmony on the back swing, there will always be too much or too little wrist break.

The perfect wrist break angle at the top of the swing is 90 degrees.

A special method of practising this is to set the wrist break angle before you swing the arms and rotate the upper body.

This will give you a very connected swing and the perfect position at the top of the swing.

From this position, which has created a coiled back swing - a dynamic down swing has a good chance of functioning.

Address position

This is the preset position just set your wrist break at 90 degrees

Rotate the upper body 90 degrees

Unwind arms and upper body

The hands and forearms release the club head

The full finish

Releasing the Club Head

There is so much talk about using the body and neutralising the hands in the golf swing.

For top professionals and elite players this can be the case as over many years of practice they have developed good hand action and in some cases need to reduce the amount of hand action in their swing.

Don`t forget they are top athletes and can use their body in a far more physical way than the average player.

Even when a top player swings there is still a release of the forearms and hands.

See position after impact in the pictures opposite.

This is a classic position everyone should strive to obtain. All the energy derived from the movements of the golf swing are released through all parts of the body and a well timed hand release. Golf is still a hand game and without knowing what the hands are doing, you will never be able to play all the short shots and special shots, which enable you to become a complete golfer.

Practice a Half Follow-Through to Develop this Position

This is a classic position everyone should strive to obtain. All the energy derived from the movements of the golf swing are released through all parts of the body and a well timed hand release.

"Keep Your Head Down" A Total Misunderstanding

How many times have you heard a player tell another player to "Keep your head down"?. If I had a pound for every time I have heard this said, I would be a very rich man indeed.

Problem- Keeping your head down causes tension, lack of mobility, broken swing arcs, short shots, mistimed shots – the list is endless.

Look at pictures 1-3, see how narrow and broken the swing has become because the head is bent against the upper chest.

Correction - The statement should read "Keep your chin up and your eyes on the ball, while allowing your neck to rotate".

This will free up the body rotation resulting in the width of swing becoming greater – both on the back swing and downswing.

This generates far more club head speed giving longer shots as a bonus - pics 4-8.

Note how after contacting the ball the head is allowed to rotate immediately after contact.

Otherwise you will not be able to continue the movement for a powerful wide & high finish.

Head down with chin touching chest

As a result arms swing without body rotation

Same result on the down swing

CORRECTION

Head held high at address

Upper body rotation begins with a wide arc

Upper body rotation finishes with a full wide back swing

A wide release of the club head is achieved

A full finish the result

Get a Grip of Your Game

Many golfers grip the club so that they feel comfortable and not in a technically correct position.

This results in many compensations during their golf swing, giving inconsistency in ball striking and direction.

Those players who take the time to learn the correct grip will benefit from straighter shots and lower scores.

A one knuckle weak grip - This will result in high, sliced and top shots.

A three knuckle strong grip - This will result in low, hooks and fat shots.

A two knuckle neutral grip - This will result in a medium trajectory, straight shots with ball turf contact.

THE TWO KNUCKLE GRIP IS THE CORRECT GRIP - DO YOU HAVE THE PATIENCE TO CHANGE?

A weak grip position, showing one knuckle on the left hand

A weak top of swing position with the bottom line of the iron in a vertical position

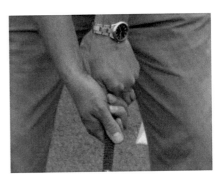

A strong grip position showing three knuckles on the left hand

A strong top of swing position with the bottom line of the iron in a horizontal position

A neutral CORRECT position showing two knuckles on the left hand

A neutral CORRECT top of swing position with the bottom line of the iron at a 22 ½ minutes past the hour position

Reverse Pivot Drill

This is for players who have a problem shifting their weight to the inside of the right leg on the back swing, leaving their weight well and truly on their left leg at the top of the back swing.

This usually results in a steep back swing with a bent left arm at the top of the back swing. There is no way of delivering a naturally powerful strike on the ball from this position.

Remedy - Lift your left heel off the ground only having ground contact with the toes. Swing the arms and rotate the upper body around a slightly bent right leg.

The transfer of the weight to the right leg will be felt immediately.

Swing back with the arms and you will feel the natural rotation of the forearms and hands delivering a solid attack on the ball.

After repeating this at least 20 times, revert to a normal stance and the movement should become automatic. If not repeat, repeat and repeat.

Lift the left heel off the ground before swinging – this sets the weight on the right leg to start with

When upper body rotation has occurred – this is the feeling you will have when pivoting correctly

This gives a good release feeling of the fore arms and hands at the impact position

6 The Modern Way of Chipping from the Edge of the Green

If you play the chip shot with a putting stroke using a seven, six or five iron with a putting grip, you will increase your level of consistency.

Grip the club like a putter - reverse overlap

Place your feet close together.

Ball position should be in the middle of your feet.

Body lines parallel to the ball to target line.

Heel of the club is off the ground.

Arms and shoulders tilt in a pendulum movement.

The toe of the club makes contact with the ball.

Especially good method when the ball lies in a hole or old divot mark.

Use a putting grip – reverse overlap – hold the putting grip in the lifelines of both hands

The heel of the putter is lifted off the ground

A side view of the pendulum movement – no hand action

A behind the line view of the pendulum movement.

Ball is contacted with the toe of the iron

Putting Practice

Putting comprises of 30%-40% of the game - ideally you should use 60% of your practice on the short game.

Use the following drill for concentration and determination.

Arrange five to ten balls in a circle and putt one after another into the hole.

If you miss one, start again until the whole circle has been completed in one sequence without missing a putt.

The balls should be a putter length from the hole. Try making it two putter lengths afterwards.

Do not go home until you have completed the session successfully.

This is a concentration drill which will help you hole
many short putts in the future

Extend Your Arms for Distance

By extending your arms on the take away you will maintain a wide arc on the back swing, resulting in very little wrist break at this point.

As you can see from the first photo, the shaft of the club is parallel to the ball to target line and at hip height.

If this wide arc is then maintained throughout the back swing, a wide arc delivery to the ball will have every chance of occurring, giving good length and accuracy.

This results in both arms extending through the ball as shown in the last photo.

A complete mirror image of the back swing position.

A wide arc is created

A wide arc is maintained

The wide arc throughout the back swing allows a healthy release and extension during the impact area.

The Plugged Ball Bunker Shot in a Medium or Shallow Bunker

Turn the toe of the club in towards yourself at an angle of 35-45 degrees - then most importantly, take your normal grip after first setting the club head position.

The stance should be square or slightly open and the shoulders parallel to the ball to target line.

The ball position should be central or a little towards the right side of your stance with your weight very slightly towards your left side.

Focus on the part of the sand you wish to make contact with - wet sand nearer the ball, softer sand further away - half an inch to two inches.

Do not hit hard as most players tend to.

When starting to make the back swing, use arms and shoulders with a maximum 90 degree wrist break.

The length of the back swing determines the length of the shot.

Start the downswing by unwinding the left arm and on impact with the sand, let the hands and club face naturally open. This action will result in the ball being dug out of its plugged position.

The ball will roll on landing on the green. However, you will be able to control the distance far better with this method than any other method.

The follow through is minimal. Do not hit hard

Turn the toe of the sand iron inwards before gripping

Shows full picture ready for action

Setting wrist action early with some upper body rotation

Unwinding arms and holding the wrist break steady

As the toe enters the sand, the club face opens popping the ball out

A short follow-through is beneficial

 **Underclubbing**

Yes we have all been guilty of the decision to think we can get the ball to fly all the way to the flag with a pitching wedge when a seven iron would more likely be the correct club.

I remember an incident in Denmark coaching the juniors on a par three hole. These were good players playing off around five handicap.

Kristian Elbo was a truly gifted player who thought he could hit the pitching wedge right up to the flag, which was situated seven metres from the back of the green.

I set a wager that if Kristian hit a normal seven iron he would finish at the back of the green. If he went over I would give him 6 top grade Titleist balls.

If on the other hand, Kristian finished on the green, he would have to pick up the driving range balls that evening for no fee.

Kristian was convinced he would easily clear the green with his seven iron.

What Kristian failed to realise was that the green was 40 metres from the front to the back - that's a difference of a minimum of four club lengths. His pitching wedge usually hit the first part of the green, so I had worked out that his seven iron would hit the back of the green.

The greens were holding that day and his shot landed in its own pitch mark three metres from the back edge.

Yes, I did pay Kristian when he picked up the practice balls later - However, Kristian seldom came up short after that episode.

Minchinhampton Old Course 18th green

Minchinhampton New Course 2nd green on the Avening Course

Both greens show how club selection varies considerably according to the pin placement especially in wet conditions when the ball stops quickly (clubs lying on ground to illustrate)

11 Your Ball is Under a Tree

How do you maximise the distance you can hit the ball when you have a restricted back swing when the ball is under a tree?

First choose a club that will get the ball into the air and low enough to miss the branches of the overhanging tree.

Then hold halfway down the grip for a controlled swing and firm contact with the ball.

Use a slightly narrower stance than normal with the weight towards the left leg - 60% to 65%. Ball should be positioned in between the middle and the right foot.

This is an arms and hands shot. The back swing must be very slow as a restricted length of swing is imposed by the branches of the tree. On the downswing you need to keep the hands in front of the club head through impact so the ball does not rise and hit the branches. Keep the hands and club head low to the ground through impact.

Remember this is a recovery shot - do not go for extreme distance.

Hold down the grip, narrow stance, weight up to 65% on left side

Make a slow & restricted back swing hinging wrist break early

This is an arms and hands shot with some rotation of the upper body keeping the hands ahead of the club face at impact

Keep the hands in front of the club head at impact so the ball stays low and doesn't` hit the branches

Turn More & Swing Less for a Coiled Back Swing

Many golfers have a long and loose back swing which results in a broken left arm and the so called over swing. This is a very loose and floppy position at the top of the back swing.

No coiling power has been generated and therefore the downswing is just a loose throw of the arms with a loss of power and direction.

This poor back swing has occurred due to the arms and hands being too active at the start of the back swing and the more powerful upper torso has been left behind.

The most common result from this is a very steep back swing with far too much wrist break and a broken left arm with a very narrow arc.

Correction - By moving the arms and body as one unit in the early stages of the back swing, the wrist break will begin around the hip height position and an upper body coiling effect will be produced, with the lower body fairly static.

Power has loaded up on the back swing ready to be released on the downswing.

No rotation of the upper body, only an arms swing, resulting in elbows bent and no radius to the swing.

A correct address position

A one piece takeaway. Upper body and arms.

Further togetherness gives a solid top of swing position with upper body coiled against the lower body

*A drill that will give
the feeling of width
and coiling*

The Downhill Lob Shot

Open the face of your sand wedge or lob wedge before gripping.

Then aim the club face(the leading edge/bottom line) at the flag or target area.

The stance and body lines will be quite open, well left of the ball to target line.

Widen the stance and have the ball towards the right foot.

Lean with the slope so the weight is predominantly on your left leg.

Wrist break early and steeply on the back swing with some upper body rotation.

Start the downswing with the left arm and upper body rotation making sure the left hand passes the ball before the club head.

This will lead the club head down the slope and although the right hand releases into the back of the ball, the club face must point to the sky at the finish, allowing the ball to pop up and land softly onto the green.

This is a high risk shot that needs plenty of practice.

Open   clubface
before gripping

Grip the club & set the club
face (bottom line) at the
ideal target

Set body lines in
an open position
with ball position
towards right

Break the wrists early and
rotate upper body with
lower body static

Unwind upper body keeping hands in front of the club head

Clubface finishes pointing to the sky and ball floats out towards target – the landing can be soft however some roll will occur according to the lie of the ball on the down slope

Use a Cross for Your Set Up

There are many golfers who practice an incorrect set-up because they just hit aimlessly, while practising.

Meanwhile others aim at a target. However, if you do not use an aid to help you set up parallel to the ball to target line, you are likely to make wrong movements to compensate for setting your body incorrectly in the first place.

What could be simpler than, after putting a ball down ready to be hit, you then line up a golf shaft parallel to the ball to target line. This will help you to set your shoulders, knees, hips and feet parallel to the ball to target line.

Then line up a second shaft at - right angles to the first shaft - this is to check that your ball position is correct in relation to your feet ie. in the middle of your feet for your iron shots.

You can then practice in the knowledge that you are set up correctly and have a great chance of producing a straight shot.

The side view shows how the ball position can be checked

The back view shows how the body can be set parallel to the ball to target line

Unplayable Lie up Against a Tree by the Side of the Green

The obvious solution in a situation like this is to take a penalty drop of one shot - read rule book for the correct procedure Rule 28.

However there are two ways of saving a shot.

Solution 1

Take your Sand Wedge and reverse the club face, taking a two handed grip for comfort. You are now in a position to play the shot left handed.

For those who feel they haven`t the ability to use this solution try solution 2

Solution 2

Stand with your back to the target and grip the sand wedge with the right hand. Swing as pictures illustrates.

If in doubt take a penalty drop - try these methods and save a shot.

Play left handed using a two handed grip

Use arms and hands with a little wrist break for longer shots

The follow through

Stand with your back facing the target

Right hand and arms make the movement

Reverse movement on down swing

38

Take the Break out of Short Putts with a Crash Putt

As soon as we have a putt of five feet and under and we can see the hole out of the corner of our eyes - the fear factor can then take over.

Players are reluctant to attack the PUTT and often see the ball dribble off to one side or the other of the hole.

If the curvature of the putt is around one to two inches to the left or right of the hole - instead of playing for the ball to roll in off the curve - hit it straight at the back of the hole.

This takes the guess work out of the borrow - curvature - simplifying the Putt.

Nick Dougherty and Thomas Bjorn are two fine exponents of this method.

You need to commit to the PUTT and be positive.

Row of balls shows curvature of the putt

Put a ball behind the hole and aim at the ball

Hit the putt very firm so the ball travels straight at the hole

17 An Exercise You Can Use at Home

Practice without a ball and learn to swing through muscular memory movements.

Stand upright with your feet together. Have both arms pointing straight out from your shoulders.

Swing arms and rotate upper body - shoulders - together in a one piece movement.

Break wrists and right elbow gradually to a 90 degree angle. Hips are pulled round to a 45 degree angle.

Start forward swing by unwinding the left arm closely followed by the upper body.

The hips will also have responded.

When the arms have moved halfway on the forward swing the forearms and wrist start to rotate squaring up the club face to its original start position.

The movement is carried through to a full release position - see last picture.

In the normal swing the whole movement will continue to a full finish - not shown.

Stand upright with club in front of you

Rotate upper body and arms through 90 degrees

Wrist break and right elbow fold 90 degrees with a little more shoulder rotation

Unwind upper body keeping the wrist break intact – hips respond

Rotate arms and wrists with continued upper body unwind – hips respond

42

18 Don`t Change Your Swing With the Driver

Many amateurs fall into the trap of thinking they must change their swing when hitting woods, compared with the irons. This is not true?

The adjustments you make to your address, stance, posture, weight position and ball position - together with the longer shaft automatically create a shallower and more rounded swing path.

All you need to do is focus on making the same movements in your swing as normal.

Swing the club away low and slow

A smooth takeaway helps to keep the club head low to the ground on the first few feet of the back swing, giving good rhythm and wide arc to the swing.

Your weight will transfer easier to the right side, leading to a full upper body rotation, resulting in a wide, powerful arc.

Do not lift the club in the air. This results in a broken narrow arc and loss of power and direction.

All six pictures show the full sequence of the golf swing with a driver and an iron being swung at the same time – When you swing the clubs together focus on the driver movement in one swing and then the iron movement in another – they will feel different because of the length of shaft and angle of the shaft - however it is the same movement that has been made

Putting Drill - Tilt the Shoulders

The correct movement of the shoulders during the putting stroke is to tilt, creating a pendulum action.

Trap a flag or the shaft of a club between your arms and chest.

During the movement if you TURN your shoulders the putter head comes way inside the line of the putt, causing directional problems on impact.

Pictures 1 & 2.

If however, you TILT your shoulders the putter head stays on line, rolling the ball towards the hole.

Pictures 3 & 4.

Shoulders turn taking putter head too far inside the ball to target line.

Shoulders turn in the opposite direction on the forward swing causing putter head to travel far too much inside again – result poor contact and direction.

Shoulders tilt keeping the putter head on the ball to target line.

A similar tilt on the forward swing keeps the putter head on the ball to target line – result a straight putt that will not deviate off line.

20 The Dreaded Shanks

In the PGA Training Manual you will find 13 ways of shanking that are normally triggered off by extreme set-up positions, such as the ball being too far forward in the stance etc.

Most shanks are caused by the club being thrown or forced outside the ball to target line on the downswing, thus resulting in contacting the ball with the neck - hosel - of the club, with the ball flying off at right angles. Fear sets in and a repeat performance is not uncommon.

The **"take a step and swing method"** will put things right.

First take your normal set up - which I hope is similar to mine.

Bring the left foot to the side of the right foot. Take a 3/4 back swing.

Take a step with the left foot back to its original position and at the same time drop the arms on the inside of the ball to target line. This forward step makes you drop the club inside as opposed to throwing the club away from you.

The result will be a contact in the middle of the club face. Problem over.

Take a normal stance

Bring the left foot to the right foot

Take a normal back swing

*Take a step forward with the left foot
as you swing down*

*A good release of the club head is achieved
through the back of the ball*

48

21 The Short 50 Yard Lob Shot

Set up the club face square - pointing at the target. Use a 60 degree Lob Wedge for extra height.

Have a slightly open stance with the shoulders parallel to the ball to target line.

Place the ball in the middle of your feet - between the middle and left heel, if the lie is very very good/lush.

Have an even weight distribution as the lie is good or very good so no need to lean onto the left side as many players do.

Hands placed over the ball or slightly in front of the ball.

Start the back swing with a pendulum action - arms and shoulders movement - breaking the wrist and right elbow 90 degrees.

Unwind the arms and body releasing the right hand, but keeping it behind the left hand.

At the finish the club head points to the sky.

Setting club face square to the target with stance square or slightly open

Ball in the middle of the stance for a good lie – even weight distribution

Upper body rotation with an early 90 degree wrist break

Lead with the arms and upper body so club face comes into contact with the ball afterwards and club face finishes pointing to the sky

50

22 Chipping When the Ball is Up Against a Collar of Rough

Having hit a reasonable shot onto the green the ball can often roll just off the green and finish up against a collar of rough. This can give problems as it is very difficult to hit the bottom of the ball and control the shot.

Fear not – use this method

By choosing a Sand Iron, 3 Wood or 2 or 3 Utility Club you can overcome the problem.

Take a putting grip (reverse overlap)

Ball position middle to slightly forward of middle

Weight level and balanced 50%-50%

Grip well down the shaft

Make a pendulum putting action, brushing the top of the grass and contact the middle of the ball.

Professionals are beginning to use the 3 Wood & Utility Clubs more than the Sand Iron, as the wide base of the clubs glides over the grass much easier than trying to hit the ball with the front (leading edge) of the Sand Iron.

With this method you can regulate the distance far easier than chopping down on the ball with the more traditional method.

Side view chipping with a metal wood

Down the line view with a metal wood

Down the line view with a metal wood showing back swing

Down the line view with a metal wood showing through swing

Side view chipping with a Sand Iron

Down the line view with a Sand Iron showing through swing

Down the line view with a Sand Iron
showing back swing

Ball Under Lip of Bunker and On the Up Slope

Most players in this situation tend to hit downwards into sand – the club gets stuck in the sand and the ball pops up into the air, rolling back into the bunker, at worst into your footprints.

This is not a good idea!!!

Take a 56 or 60 degree Sand Iron according to the distance required. Use a square club head position at address. Aim right of the target, the club head closes as you swing up the slope.

Swing up the slope taking some sand and really accelerating the club head through the sand. The ball will swing from right to left coming back to the flag or target.

Remember this is a damage limitation exercise and if the ball is under the lip, you can always take a one shot penalty under the unplayable rule 28, rather than hitting the ball further into the sand and compounding the problem.

Lean with the slope

Setting the wrist break

Unwinding and swinging up the slope

Side view address

Side view wrist break

Side view unwinding and swinging up the slope

24   A Tree or Bush is in the Way of My Ball and the Green

Playing round a tree or bush - Sometimes in this situation you can play round the left or right of the obstacle. If you are too close to the tree or bush, then it is best to play sideways. This of course results in the loss of a stroke.

Another solution – play over – with what club?

To find the club that will give you maximum length and land as near to the green as possible, take the next steps.

Stand on the face of the iron you think will clear the obstacle.

Follow the extension of the shaft and if it clears the obstacle – you can use that club.

However if the line of the shaft will hit part of the obstacle, so will the ball when struck.

Therefore take a club with a higher number on it until the line of the shaft clears the obstacle.

The outcome – a possible shot saved.

NO trajectory too low

NO trajectory too low

YES trajectory high enough to clear bushes

YES trajectory high enough to clear bushes

Calculating Distances With Your Irons

How many times have I listened to my pupils telling me they have hit a seven iron 190 yards. I`m thinking, "if I had hit shots that far, I would be on the European Tour and be in the top 50 in the world".

Golfers do have Visions of Grandeur.

The best way to calculate the distance you hit the ball is to wait for a calm day and hit 30 balls on the practice area on level ground.

Use the same type of balls that you play with on the course - otherwise you will get a distorted reading.

A 7 iron is recommended.

The flight of the ball should be so that on landing the ball rolls only a few yards.

If your ball is rolling a long way or spinning sideways, book a lesson!

Having hit your 30 shots - pace out to the middle of the circle you have created.

Swing sequence

Swing sequence

Hit 30 shots and take an average length of the shots

Stride out in yards or metres

Pace to the centre of the circle of balls for correct measurement

60

26 Separation is The Secret to a Successful Downswing

In my humble opinion many teachers and players have fallen into the trap of thinking that by working the upper body more and neutralising the hands the striking of the ball will be more consistent.

This can be the case for the top Professional who have well trained hands after many years on the practice ground, hitting millions of shots. However, even they produce a separation at the start of the down swing to get themselves into a position where they can release the club head with the forearms , hands and YES the upper body on the ball to target line.

The average player who tries to unwind the upper body at the start of the down swing will often find they move the club head outside the ball to target line resulting in the ball starting left of target. The player who unwinds in a similar way but keeps the arms close to the body on the down swing will find the club head not squaring up and blocking the shot to the right of target. There are several other scenarios but these two examples are the most common.

What is Separation?

I am assuming you are all in a good position at the top of the swing. As you can see from the address position and top of swing position - the hands have come closer to the right shoulder through the hinging of the wrists on the back swing.

Therefore on the down swing the hands and arms have further to travel on their journey to connect with the ball than the upper body. Therefore they have to start fractionally ahead of the upper body - THAT`S SEPARATION.

The Separation Movement

By unwinding the arms and hands fractionally ahead of the upper body and keeping the 90 degree wrist break intact until the arms arrive level with the hips you are now in a position to release the forearms, hands and upper body, thus producing maximum club head speed and good direction

The top of swing position ready for the separation to take place

The arms and hands unwind a fraction ahead of the right shoulder – that is what is meant by separation

62

27 Beware of Pitch Marks on The Fringe, Fore Green or Semi Green

I remember an article in the December edition of Golf Monthly about Bart Bryant. It reminded me of an even greater outcome from a similar incident in a Club Championship at Gilleleje Golf Club in Denmark, where I was Professional for 12 years.

Eric Ravn, an up and coming Junior, playing off 5 handicap was well placed in the 1st round. He was from memory only a few shots over par coming down the par 5 18th hole. His 3rd shot landed just off the green leaving him a few metres from the flag.

His playing partner had played first and landed a yard in front of where Eric`s ball had come to rest, making a pitch mark and just running onto the green.

When Eric arrived at the green he repaired the pitch mark that his playing partner had made and proceeded to chip on to the green and make his par. The scores were checked signed and delivered to the match room.

A player having lunch on the veranda had remarked that the pitch mark was already there before Eric`s ball landed and therefore Eric had breached Rule 13-2 by improving his line of play by eliminating irregularities on the ground (even though Eric had chipped over the pitch mark).

Normally this would give Eric a 2 shot penalty - however Eric had returned his scorecard to the match room - the only outcome was to disqualify Eric.

This was a very unusual incident as Eric was a very honest player and had repaired the pitch mark in good faith.

So beware next time you see a pitch mark just short of the green.

Procedures for repairing pitch (ball) marks

Pitch marks off the putting green may not be repaired if doing so would improve the position or lie of the ball, the area of intended swing or stance, the line of play or the area in which the ball is to be dropped or placed.

A pitch mark that is on the putting green may be repaired at any time, regardless of where the players ball lies.

If a ball is accidentally moved when repairing a pitch mark on the green, there is no penalty as long as the movement was directly attributed to the act of repairing the pitch mark - the ball is replaced. **REMEMBER TO HAVE A RULE BOOK IN YOUR BAG AT ALL TIMES – MANY SHOTS WILL BE SAVED BY DOING SO.**

The pitch mark in front of the ball is another player's and is not on the green (not clearly defined in the picture) and cannot be repaired.

28 The 10 Yard Rule

Most people come off the course after a Tournament Round completely shattered. The reason being they have played a four and a half hour round of golf and during the round they are thinking of how they have hit this and that shot - thinking of how many shots they are over par - how they should have done better on hole eleven - worrying about hole sixteen which is their bogey hole - if only they hadn't three putted the fourth hole etc. WE HAVE ALL DONE IT!!!!.

Its easy to play good golf when the shots are flying straight at the flags - this type of round happens once a year if your lucky.

Therefore how can we concentrate better on a golf course so we are still fresh for the last shot and putt on the 18th hole.

Dr. Carl Morris in his CD Train The Brain talks about the 10 yard rule and how this action can help save you energy and mental frustration thus resulting in better scores.

Take Action

Paint a piece of wood in your favourite colour and place it 10 yards in front of every shot that you play on the course during your next round (excluding tournaments, competitions & putts).

After every shot you can express your feelings to yourself about the outcome of the shot (try not to go ballistic if its a very wayward shot). After you get to the piece of wood, pick it up and while walking to the ball for the next shot, don't think of anything to do with GOLF.

Look around and enjoy the countryside, talk to your partners about tonight's activities, other sports etc. but do not mention GOLF.

Only when you get to your ball do you again begin to think about your next shot, after putting the piece of wood 10 yards ahead of your ball.

This exercise can take up to 7 rounds of play before it becomes second nature and you can dispense with the piece of wood.

Better energy levels and a clear mind over the shot in hand will be the outcome of this exercise and this will give better results on the scorecard.

Driving off the tee with the piece of wood 10 yards in front of the tee.

Hitting the second shot from the middle of the fairway again with the piece of wood 10 yards in front of the player.

A Transportation Shot

Many players who have hit their tee shot into the rough take a gamble and try to hit the green on a par four with their second shot although their ball is lying deep in the grass.

I have seen players trying to hit 3 irons out of the rough with the result that the ball moves a few yards as the grass turns the club head leaving no angle on the face to get the ball airborne.

The rescue clubs have been a great help as they brush through the grass and therefore have a better chance of flying the ball towards the target. Even the rescue clubs have no chance in certain situations and you can even be playing a Sand Iron just to get yourself back on the fairway.

When in this situation PLAY A TRANSPORTATION SHOT - In other words choose a club that will safely get you back on the fairway. This will set you up for an easier third shot to the green with a chance of saving par. By gambling to hit a longer second shot you may end up still playing your third shot from the rough and scoring a double bogey or higher.

Practice playing from the rough with a Sand Iron, Pitching Wedge, 9, 8 and 7 iron etc. and see what reaction the ball has from various positions with various irons. Then you will know your limitations.

Situation

Ball in deep rough - Select an iron for maximum control - in this instance a Sand Iron - target area selected to give third shot a better chance of success - make a steep swing with plenty of early wrist break - pull downwards with the left hand and arm steeply into the back of the ball - obtain as much ball contact as possible - this should pop the ball into the air sending it towards your chosen target.

DO NOT GAMBLE & KEEP YOUR SCORE TO A MAXIMUM OF A BOGEY

*Ball in deep rough-
Select an iron for
maximum control*

*Target area selected to
give third shot a better
chance of success*

*Taking aim on the
safe line*

*Make a steep swing
with plenty of early
wrist break*

Peter Dangerfield

Pull downwards with the left hand and arm steeply into the back of the ball – make a firm contact with the back of the ball.

Side view showing ball is back in the stance

Steep back swing with early wrist break

Firm contact with the ball and a curtailed follow through

The Punch, Knock Down Shot or Tiger Woods Stinger

This is an abbreviated half or 3/4 swing both on the back swing and down swing in which the priority is total control of the shot resulting in a low trajectory.

Reasons for playing this shot

1. To keep the ball low under the wind.

2. When the distance you require is in between clubs (ie. 5 or 6 iron then take a soft 5 iron).

3. To decrease the amount of spin on the ball, so you can play the shot with more precision.

4. Playing fast running links fairways, where you need to land the ball short of the green and yet have the ball bounce forward towards the hole.

5. On certain holes where there are many hazards around the green, this type of shot can give control and direction. A safety shot of the highest calibre.

6. The Tiger Woods Stinger is often played off the tee in adverse weather conditions; again primarily for position and safety.

Club Selection

Always take 1 or 2 clubs more than normal (ie. if the distance would normally be a 7 iron, then take a 5 or 6 iron or even in extreme conditions a 4 iron.

The Technique

Ball position between the middle of the stance and the right (back) foot.

Hands are automatically well forward of the club head because of the ball position.

Weight slightly forward on the left side at address to help squeeze the shot.

As previously stated a calm 1/2 to 3/4 back swing with the hands not passing shoulder height and a similar follow through position.

Play percentage golf and you could save yourself a few shots per round.

Ball position between the middle of the stance and the right (back) foot.

A calm 1/2 to 3/4 back swing with the hands not passing shoulder height and a similar follow through position. This action will keep the ball down under the wind with great control

Behind the ball to target line view